In Memory of
James E. Best

Dedicated to the 3 most important folks in my life
Doris J. Best
James C. Best
Robert L. Ellerbe-Jones

Thank you all for the love and constant inspiration

Of Love: The Poetry of Rare Epiphany

ISBN 978-0-578-01834-8

Of Love...

Chapters:

Love~Inspired~

Pieces:

When You're Gone — For My Friend's friend

Tony — For DeWayne (Tony) Thompson

Marcia — For Marcia Woods-Hines

For Luther — For Luther Vandross

A Stitch in Time made Nyne — For NyneElementz

Nina — For Nina Simone

A Blues For Phyllis — For Phyllis Hyman

Jamie — For James Christopher Best

Doris Jean — for my mommy

For Tasha — For Tasha

Always — For Shannon Leigh

Love ~ Found~

Pieces:

Love Song

In On With

He Made Love to Me ~783~

Cooling Waters

I Just Want You To Love Me

Moonsong

Was It Something I Said?

Memory

Come ~InSide~

The Mender

Love ~ Lost~

Pieces:

Encore

Of Love

The Hours

Love TKO

Levity

Gone

Spring Cleaning

Cry

Assignment Piece # 1

Assignment Piece #2 – Why (Never)

Make You Free

Love ~Self~

Pieces:

No More Tears

Independence Day ~Woman In The Mirror~

Somewhere

Love Rains

Now Found ~ The Woman I Could Be~

The Blessing of Writer's Block

Inside Out

Hairycane

In The Doing ~ Dancing At Night~

10 minutes 'til Midnight ~Dam won't break~

They Thought They Knew Me ~ Ego Trippin' Pt. 2

Love ~Making~

Pieces:

Home ~ The Deep Down of Me~

Lick ~Handle~

Can't Hide Love

Just Breathe

Memory Lane

Body Music

Nights Like This

He's Cumming For Me

Mind Grindin'

The Kiss

Again

Love

Inspired

When You're Gone

For My Friend's Friend

When you're gone...

I'll whisper 'goodnight' to your fading image on the mental screens of my mind

I'll sigh and laugh my way through the inevitable tears and heartbreak

When you're gone.

When you're gone...

I'll hold my friend really tight even though we don't do that girly type stuff

And I'll tell her it's going to be alright although I know "alright" doesn't mean "all good"

It just means it won't hurt so much one day and you learn to live with that

Ball of dark emptiness that forms in your gut

I'll remember with her and hurt with her

When you're gone...

I'll share the stories

Ask the questions

Wonder at the unfairness of it all

Curse, cry, and scream

Pray until something in me breaks

Resign the wrongful anguish of your life to the list of questions I'm gonna ask God when It's my turn to sit at His feet

I promise you I will do it all

When you're gone

But right now, you are here

In pain but HERE

Broken but HERE

Going but NOT GONE!!!!

So I will fight for you

I will pray for you

I will stand in front of God and humanity begging for a cure

Not just for cancer

But for abuse and pain and rape and hate

I will hold on until there is nothing left to hold on to

I won't let you go

I won't let you go

I WON'T LET YOU GO!!

….until you are gone

It's not over yet

I'm the fat lady

And I'm not ready to sing

There'll be time enough for that

When you're gone…

Tony ~ For Tony Thompson

He is the wand in God's hand

Used to stir up the gifts

And uplift the carriers of heavy burdens

No magic in his means

Just a keen ear for the Master's melody

Supernaturally

As if he lay his head upon the very bosom of Christ

~The Maestro from on High~

Then turns the lullabies he hears there into love songs

that we can offer up to God's throne

in practiced and perfecting tones

Letting it be known that excellence is a requirement

And not an option

We owe too much for our adoption into the family of the King

To bring just anything

So Tony demands our very best

Puts our talent and proclivities to the test every time we open our mouths

Whether in rehearsal or a concert hall

He expects you to give your all

Because God is the real audience

So it only make sense that we bless him in the choir room

Just like we do in the sanctuary

See worship is not some arbitrary action or task

Ask Tony...He knows!

That when one goes before the Almighty

You must stand uprightly and bring forth

A joyful noise

And stand before Christ poised for a miracle

That transcends just some lyrical rendering

It takes your EVERYTHING.

You've got to raise your hands as well as your voices

Stomp your feet until the building rejoices

Praise is an activity of the Mind, Heart Body and Spirit

And it should move the souls of those who hear it.

Be it Hymn or Spiritual

Anthem or Gospel

The music gets inside Tony regardless of label

And then it moves through his limbs and the smile on his face

The infectiousness of the anointing becomes apparent in the place

And in that sacred space in time, he bids us all to find the awesomeness of grace

In that we are even allowed to come before a Righteous God

When all that we are is clearly at odds with His goodness

Tony just…blesses us that we might, in turn, bless the Lord

He teaches us to use our instrument with all the power and skill we can afford

He is the wand in God's hand

Used to stir up the gifts

So it's only fitting that today we come to uplift

Him

Marcia

She is…

The sunlight glistening from the center of a raindrop

The calm encapsulated in the storm

Her warmth radiates & kisses everything in her range

She is…

The strange fruit reborn & birthed through time & tears

Blossoming then, ripening, into

Lush; firm sweetness

Feeding & nourishing her fellowman

She is…

The song sung in the midnight

When the will to fight is lost

But her lyrics bid you to hold on

'cause trouble don't last too long

She is…

The bridge o'er the void;

Standing in the gap

Wrapping your woes in prayers

Like a mother swaddling her young

Yet, going unsung

Content to be the wind beneath wings

She is so many things…

A teacher; a mentor

A wife & mother

A daughter & sister

~No we will never forget her brothers~

But as for me and my house

She is...

The sunlight glistening from the center of a raindrop

The gold at the rainbows' end

Confidante

Comfort

Ram in the thicket

Woman of God & Friend

For Luther

His music is

forever

not some clever rhyme scheme to shake things up for a minute

he's in it for the long run

The kinda music that makes you hum love songs in the midst of tears

day after day and year after year

He sang sweetly

like honey from the comb

and long after this generation is gone

THE Balladeer will live on 'cause

His music is

For Always

crackling lovely off vinyl or squeaking easy off cassette

setting the mood for rump shaking and baby making

at the same time

Melodies so fierce that they will pierce the ears

of our children's children's children

drilled in immortal symphony in the ways of

Sam Cooke and Donny Hathaway.....

Jackie Wilson and Marvin Gaye

His music is

For Love

whether backseat creepin'

or romance you fall deep in

his voice just crept in and moved you

on the inside

bypassed pride and opened you wide to the possibility

to the vulnerability

to the urgency of love

rich baritone groans that made contact a necessity

and believe you me, when Luther's playing

it's no myth

If you can't be with the one you love, it'll make you love the one you're with

and thank God above we were blessed with an oak tree

that will shade us with song for eternity

Luther Vandross was

but his music IS

forever

for always

for love

A Stitch in Time Made Nyne ~ For Nyne Elementz ~

He was Iced Fire

And I was blessed to feel the cool of his flame

When icicles sparked indigo from his pen

See even then

Minds were left frostbitten

In the wake of his writtens

Words so hot from a brotha so cold

Truth be told we weren't ready

So he waited on bated breath until fear left a void wide enough

For the real stuff

That nitty grit that he could spit cool into mics

And morph molten to melt speaker wires

The coldest fire ever felt

Melting minds frozen from the dozing induced by complacency

Coaxed them to taste and see that knowledge is the nectar of the gods

Then, shod in wisdom, he'd soon become more than the polar extremes

But deemed ennead

Strengthened and clad by the ancients in the garments of priesthood

To speak good into the hooded eyes of a blinded people who will sequel

The sins of the past unless taught to go off script

Equipping them with enough history to recognize the trickery

And bitchery in the version of "free" we've been served

Let the truth be heard

The universe proudly presents

Nyne Elementz

So beware 'cause ignorance now has no defense

And intolerance for lack of recompense is the consequence of knowing

And knowing

Is beautiful

Nina

For Nina Simone

She was an oak tree among weeping willows

and her silhouette danced against the night sky

high above the petty proclivity to sell ones soul to the devil for fame

for a name in an industry hell-bent on producing cookie-cutter clutter

that butters the bread of big men smoking in easy chairs

She dared speak a word of truth

to the adults and youth of our world

this girl-flower bloomed into woman-vine

entwining us in wisdom.

Defined herself as "little one"

who's gentle drum called black hearts in the night

bidding dreams, `take flight'

urging complacency into fight

beating wrongs into right

didn't bite her tongue

and among the brilliance that flowed from her fingertips

came reassurance from her lips that I was

Young, gifted, and black

Lacked nothing due to my hue

but was imbued with greatness.

She paints this picture...with sound....

and creates music with silence

Didn't sugar-coat hard realities of

racism, sexism and violence

She was honest and she knew what she stood for

and wasn't afraid to vacate this place when her spirit could take no more.

It was 1974 when she freed herself to take flight

and that might have destroyed some, but not this queen

her dream lived on; still lives on in the yellowed scores of yesteryears

in the haunting way of all pioneers and...

She was...

an oak tree among weeping willows

and her silhouette danced against the night sky

high above the petty proclivity to sell ones soul to the devil for fame

for a name in an industry hell-bent on producing cookie-cutter clutter

that butters the bread of big men smoking in easy chairs

She dared speak a word of truth

to the adults and youth of our world

this girl-flower bloomed into woman-vine

entwining us in wisdom and her kingdom

Lives On.

A blues for Phyllis ~Middle Place~

for Phyllis Hyman

I live out loud on stages

Belting out my sorrows like

Lava from Vesuvius mouth

Its all guts and glory

And my blood drips from each line

My life's work is to lay myself bare

Beneath scrim lights

fighting a losing battle for my sanity

while cold voyeuristic souls huddle close

to the heat of my struggle

they gasp and pray

curse and sway

and somewhere in my wounds they find healing

I fall...spent and broken to the floor

they raise their voices and clap their hands

stand to their feet and smile

content to walk away

filled

while I lay

empty

who sings for the singer?

They clamor at the dressing room door

~Everybody wants a piece~

But I've already given my all

And while they snatch at the scraps of me

Loneliness weaves itself into the crowd

Flashing that knowing look

Shouting above the accolades

Tonight its you and me baby

and my smile belies the fear burgeoning in my throat

like gall

threatening to erupt into maniacal screams

~home~

Where the stillness breaks my bones

Crushed beneath the weight of this loneliness

I find it hard to breathe

I got nothing in the middle

And the fragile pieces of me fall apart

I got both ends of extreme running games in my head

A wretch undone am I

And this bitter brew I can no longer drink

So I lay me down in the silence

til what the doctor ordered

ushers me into everlasting peace

cet endroit de milieu

that middle place

Jamie

for James Christopher Best ~my son~

Staring, transfixed, into the night

Trying to catch a glimpse of heaven

I spy a shooting star

my eyes close

But no wishes come to mind

And I close my window with a smile

Reminded , once again as I look into your sleeping face

That I have no need to search the sky for heaven

I have it right here in you

Doris Jean

N

ever had to wonder.

.....If you loved me

      or you cared.

         If you would answer when I called

            or understand my tears when I cried

      I never had to wonder

N

ever once doubted

    you'd listen to my ramblings

    laugh at my jokes

        pick me up when I fell

        stand by me when I faltered

      I never, once, doubted because…

Y

ou loved me.

        when I didn't love myself

believed in me

        when the world said I couldn't

  supported me

       even when it meant you had to go without

You loved and sacrificed for me.

A

nd I appreciate what you have been to me

and I love you … with a deep, abiding love

and I want you to know that although I was a

            Daddy's Girl

      I am my

          Mother's Woman

         -a product of the nurturing power of a strong

         beautiful, proud, determined black woman.

I

am a reflection of all that you are, and for that most precious of blessings from God, I am eternally grateful. It is my honor and privilege to be the daughter of James Edward and…

Doris Jean

For Tasha

~ my sister I couldn't save ~

Mama told me that someday

somebody would love me.

She said that there was somebody for everybody

and that he would think that I

Me..

that I was beautiful.

Mama told me that somebody

would think that I was the most

talented and intelligent and kind

woman that they had ever met.

She told me that he would laugh at my jokes

and never hurt me and want to be with me

always

That's what my mama told me

But she never told me that

I would fall deeply and hopelessly in love with another man

One who couldn't love me

who found me amusing as a friend and lover

but not quite what he wanted in a wife.

She never said that I would

cry myself to sleep at night

and develop a nervous laughter whenever

he walked into a room…

never said that I would be jealous and vengeful

She never told me that the man I loved

wouldn't be the man that loved me.

Mama never told me that I would

sit for hours alone

waiting...waiting for the phone to ring or

familiar knocking on the door...

She never said I would sit and rock

staring aimlessly into space wondering

what the hell was wrong with me

wonder why he couldn't find it in his heart to love me

Mama never once said that I would

spend hundreds of hours and thousands of dollars

in therapy , reclining in the pristine offices of specialists

pontificating upon the finer parts of my insanity

she never said I would need mental health days and that

I'd have to figure out ways to explain the scars on

my wrists and "accidental" overdoses;

the ruptured blood vessels in my eyes

and the involuntary tremor that I've developed.

She never told me that I would try to

change who I was in order to be

who he needed and wanted.

Thanks for filling my head with dreams

that actualized into nightmares called

reality.

Now my whole messed-up existence

revolves around what she never told me..

now I know that something must be wrong with me

because if you knew all of this, she most certainly

would have told me…wouldn't she?

Mama?

Always

~For Shannon Leigh ~

You may not know her but you feel ~she~

word warrior wielding a tongue of fire

spitting the desires and diatribes of her people; all people

on stages and in venues

Continued to astound the ancient world with her

20 years of wisdom

no dumb blonde here no

a substantive sister with the gift of gab

and an extensive vocab

that she used in her lab to create mellifluous word art

that would impart some smarts

into the minds of the listeners

miss her....

but not her message

mourn her

but lose not the vestiges of her life

strife makes you strong

don't tarry too long in one place

lift your face to the sun from another country

Converse with God from the sod of a foreign land

while striving to understand him through all his people

Equally

You...feel ~she~

Though you may not know her

and even now that she's gone

her words will live on

always

Love

Found

Love Song

I want to be your love song.

I want to be the humming of birds that wakes you in the morning

The beating of your heart with each new day that's dawning

Your wanton whispered melody

Your emancipation cry of jubilee

I want to be your love song

I want to be the shrill and screaming blues song that moves you to tears

The low and steady Gregorian chant that carries you through distant years

I want to be your lingering lyrical line; the star to which you croon

I want to be the didactic, boom to bip; that rim shot in your improvisational tune

I want to be your love song….

I want to be that work song that brings unity to a heart of discord

I want to be the bridge over troubled water song sent to comfort you straight from the Lord

I want to be that melody that sustains you when you're riding through the storm

That ditty you hum when you're whole world seems safe and warm

I want to be your love song

I want to be that…that song that keeps you sane when you thought you would lose your mind

That peace-giving, hard-living, wipe the tears that stain your pillow kind.

I want to be that melody that makes you nod your head and close your eyes

The one that makes you think of velvet waters and an orange-yellow sunrise

That ethereal moan of ecstasy that emanates from deep inside you

I want to be that walking on air lullaby that woos you when I'm there beside you

I want to be your love song

Sing me, scream me, moan me, breathe me

Play me, hum me, belt me, feel me

I need to be your chorus and bridge and change

Sweeping lines that span from the top to bottom of your range

Hypnotize and Harmonize

Crescendo, glissando, Synthesize

I want to be your symphony, aria, variation in fugue

Movement, cantata, midnight bird-like groove

I just want to be

I just need to be

Please let me be your

Love song.

In ~ On ~ With

In the whisper of evening breezes

That paint the sky in the scattered earth-tones of leaves fallen from Mother's Nature's crown

I hear you

On the cusp of the horizon;

in the cool purples that lay draped in layers of blue

wrapped lovingly around sun and moon

I see you

With the faint murmur of words pushed through smiling lips

And the warmth and desire of sentiments unspoken yet palpable and clear

With pen and paper; heart and soul

I pray that you hear me

And see me

too

783 (He Made Love To Me)

He made love to me

from 783 miles away

They say that a picture is worth

a thousand words

but I blindly heard

each syllable

and the visual display his

po-e-tre'

projected upon the screens of my mind

was equivalent to a slow grind

hitting my mental g-spot

believe it or not

he touched me in places no man had

ever touched before

touched places I didn't know existed; left me satisfied

yet hungry for more

see...he took my dreams

and in delicate keystrokes

made them all come true

took tired neglected romance

and made it wondrously brand new.

he took the time to explore my mind

and peer inside my soul

patiently waded through my resistance

didn't take, but let me relinquish control

He courted me

I mean seriously set out to win my heart

bypassed all the silly games...my God yall where do I start?

He holds my hand and takes me for long walks

has never once complained about our all-night talks

shamelessly kisses me in public places

murmurs "I love you" on a regular basis

He dances with me under the moonlit tapestry of the sky

cradles me 'round the small of my back and looks me in my eyes

and tells me that I'm beautiful in a timbre so sweet

then sings with Stevie about how my love knocks him off his feet

My baby runs his fingers through my thick black tresses

pulls me close and shyly confesses the secrets of his soul

reveals the hopes and fondest dreams he's never ever told

ooh and he feeds me a meal he's lovingly prepared

shares flirtatious glances that make me keenly aware of my femininity

within me he...he dissipates the darkness and hardness that had taken hold

takes my broken, mishapened heart and slowly begins to mold it into the image of the Almighty

giving me the strength to love again

and just when I think it can't get any better, he takes me by my hand

leads me to a candlelit room

roses and vanilla incense create love's most potent perfume

He sits and beckons me to the space between his thighs

I smile in deepest anticipation and kindly; sublimely oblige

I lean back and rest my

head on his chest

relishing his warm breath

in my hair

and there, he held me all night long

and when the beauty of the moment overwhelmed me

he guided me into calm

with feather-light kisses

tells me this is a place of safety

then he lays me down and, like Whitney sang,

rocks me slow

and he made love to me

from 783 miles away

and we never had to take off our clothes...

Coolin' Waters (thirsty no more)

As Lazarus was to the rich man

so are you to me

My hope of relief from this place of abandon

In you, my spirit flies free

Put your finger in the water, come and cool my tongue

'cause I'm tormented in the flame

the acrid heat of this solitude

waxed cold when you spoke my name

You flooded my heart with inspiration

came crashing upon my shores with joy

Beaded and saturated my heart like condensation

a slow rippling I could not ignore

Held me closely; cocooned in your depths

and step by step lonely lost its grip...

and it's like coolin' waters

It feels just like coolin' waters on my soul

it's like coolin' waters

it feels just like coolin' waters on my soul

My life was a desert place

barren and bare

but still without hesitation

you set up residence there

sought out and discovered my oasis

cultivated life anew

muddied yourself to replant my gardens

but baby you weren't through

You conjured up a gentle breeze

and then evaporated like dew

gathered yourself in billowy clouds

and in my darkest places you grew

Set forth a rumbling and shaking

thunder clap and lightening sharp

then rained down love in torrential floods

cleansed and purged every part

...and I fought – not recognizing that you were my salvation

I struggled – not understanding these chilly sensations

then I let go – was encompassed by a sweet elation

and with patience...patience

you taught me to love me and gave me sweet ecstasy...

and it's like coolin' waters

It feels just like coolin' waters on my soul

it's like coolin' waters

it feels just like coolin' waters on my soul

I just want you to love me…

the way that Adam loved Eve

Like David loved Bathsheba

the way Nelson loved South Africa

enough to forfeit freedom

I need a…

devotion like

Jacob's….when he slaved to win his Rachel

and even when tricked and given Leah

he kept working for his true angel

I want your pulse to race at sight of me

your heart to increase its beating

your mouth to go dry and your palms to sweat

like men did in the presence of Nefertiti

I need thee

to love me

like

the Shulamite woman did Solomon

the way the Father loved His only Son

the way a thirsty soul loves water

the way daddy's love their only daughters

Love me so deeply

that it will consume me

drown me in its purity

blind me til I can't see

and I promise

I will love you in return

with a passion and fervor that hotly burns

I will love you like Angela Davis loved the revolution

love you as deeply as the Sphinx's convolution

Adore you the way that Cyrano De BerGerac adored Roxane

Care for you the way Mother Theresa revered her fellow man

You are my hero and my king

the love song I was born to sing

To you I give my mind, my soul, and my body freely

and all I need in return is just for you to love me.

MoonSong (Black on Black)

He wore black beautifully

Like he was the sky and

Nighttime was his ready black robe

Righteousness

Personified

Eyes sparklin like new money

Stars blingin tastefully round his neck

And dangling from each ear

His voice was a full moon

Drawing me into the inky blackness of his embrace

And I cant wait for each days blues to deepen

Into indigo and deeper still into the coal black

That kisses his skin goodnight each lunar dawning

My sensual Celestial Sultan

To whom I submit willingly

Loving me cosmic

til my astral orbit is disrupted

and I am flung deep so deep so deeply

into the outer limits of his mental

that breath is an afterthought

and sight is a primordial memory

and all around me is blackness; his blackness

his mocha soul glow

bathing me blind to any other colors

and

bathing me invisible to any other brothas

I

Now interstellar lover

No longer earthbound

Sing his praises throughout the universe

cause he wears black beautifully

inside

and out

And has wisdom enough to recognize

So do I

Was It Something I Said?

My old flame asked me if I was still in love

Wanted to know if the vacancy he'd left after his eviction was still sufficiently filled

Not like he wanted to move his furniture back in, but more like

he wanted to feel missed

but you know I can't lie. So I tried to changed the subject but he just

wouldn't let it be so I smiled…inhaled deeply and told him.

I told him all about you.

'bout how your kisses are like strawberries

Soaked in sugar water for jam

Stickywetjuiciness

Too decadent for constant consumption

But much too delicious to resist

Giggled,"…boy if I don't stop, I'mma be wearing that brotha on my hips…"

Told him

Your tongue is like lava

Making a slow hot descent down my slopes

Taking my curves slow …easy

Cause you know it's dangerous

I mean you could slip and just…

Slide up into something… if you don't watch yo'self

And…and

I explained that

Your voice is like Coltrane's Equinox

Slithering smooth and electric through my veins

Painting me with melody from the inside out

Giving me no other choice but to sing you

In honeyed moans that bloom

From my soul and leave the fragrant

Aroma of your name on my breath

...

And then...well then he left

It was the darned'st thing

I mean..was it something I said?

Hmm

I Guess...

Memory

It's been 10 months

And 10 days

Since I last beheld his smile

And all that while, it still refracts light in the darkest recesses of my mind

Time has slipped like sand betwixt the seconds and minutes and hours since my lungs were blessed to share the same air as he

But me, I still smell the warm fragrance of his skin

In the morning breeze

And with familiar ease, my mind rewinds and replays every phrase that left his lips

Those soft sweet lips

that sipped my kisses slow

Like vintage Chateau Palmer Troisieme Cru Classe Margaux 1945

Tried and succeeded in binding me tighter, still in the web of his love

Covered me in a blanket of serenity I'd relegated to the imaginative whim of some dreamer

And though it's been

10 months

And 10 days

Since I laid eyes on that man

Understand that he takes my breath away

Daily

and maybe…just maybe

in our time apart, my heart can grow more worthy of the

sacred kind of love he extends to me

and then I can be the reality whose memory

keeps him coming back for more.

Come ~ Inside ~

My borders are opened

And my doors flung wide

Tides roll in slowly

And wholly

my welcoming shores bid thee to

Come

The span of my arms

And breadth of my hips

Slip 'round your frame

Lips whisper your name

Sweetly

Tenderly

Like last dying words

Like savored last kisses

This is...

An invitation

To build nations in the kingdom of my womb

Love, like Lazarus, is risen from the tomb

Rehobath, I am your gift that maketh room

For thee

So feel free to

Come

The gates of my mind

Swing open on hinges of

Hope and

Passion

My desire fashioned by your

Warm hand

Soft yet demanding

And singing is ringing

From my very bones

You alone have entered the secret chambers of my soul;

Control it as if on marionette strings

And joy brings on gossamer wings

My solitary plea

For thee to

Come

Palms splayed

Moist from all my days

Spent praying

Praying that your ship, in the grip

Of nightfall, might just call

My lighthouse home

And maybe

One day see fit to adorn

The walls of my future

With pictures framed in your essence

And in the presence of the universe

We, two, traverse time and space as one

So, again, I bid Thee

Come

For day is dying

And trying to live in the night

Without you as my light is a futile mission

with no provisions for my breaking heart

And things fall apart when I'm alone

I want to know and be known by you

I want to experience the sweetest bliss avec tu

What's a wanting soul to do

But softly bid you to

Come

The Mender (UnSelfish)

He came upon her shattered heart

and gathered all the pieces

flung them into the heavens

against an inky black sky

deeming them stars fit to adorn the night

and then He watches

admiring his handiwork

content to simply

bear witness to her glow

Love

Lost

Encore

He was ..comfortable

like an old shoe

or

cherished pair of sweats

and I guess my knack for

straightforwardness just may have trespassed

on his piety ...or

it could be a variety of things

it just seems that between us

things have changed

such a shame

'cause he became my cloud 9

where I could recline in safety

he made me feel warm

like breezes on summer days

and the ways that he touched me

without touching me still leave me amazed

cocooned me lavishly in robes of read

suspended me in animation with each word he said

poured his heart like libations in the conduit of my ear

and swept clear all matter that didn't matter 'cause there was no place for it here

Not my lover in any physical sense

but on a mental and spiritual level so much more intense

Many were convinced that it had to manifest in sex and that vexed his soul.

I simply ignored all that chatter 'cause I refuse to let the simple control the boundlessness of the inner rest in our in-te-rest

in each other

My mother taught me long ago

that what folk don't know or fully understand

They seek to destroy out of their own self lack

and they do everything they can

to turn something so pure and blessed

into some unholy mess

'til the stress of explaining the reality

just completely depletes your soul

…they stole my summer breeze

and the easy conversation has ceased to flow

like milk and honey

Funny how

yesterdays quickly fall away into fond memories

and shimmery futures ripple wildly off center

when enters the pebbles of jealousy

and other debris

on the tranquil sea that was us

and…

now my cloud 9 doesn't hold me any more

but I see rain on the horizon

so I await

an encore.

Of Love

What I dream of love…is long talks in the park

and watching the sunset; reveling in light merging into dark

what I dream of love is violins and silly grins and dancing

I dream of toes wiggling on sandy beaches with high tides slowly advancing

and in my dreams, love is deep and wide and strong and everlasting

and in my dreams, love is a holy sacrament like prayer and fasting

Love is beautiful and it flows freely in languid pools of amber

Love is prose and poetry – free-verse and iambic pentameter

In my dreams, love helps me grow and continually nurtures me

and love never fails to accept me as I am while still guiding me into maturity

that's what I dream of love.

But

What I know of love is that I love too fast and too hard

and I know that I have never held hands at all

never known love to send me flowers at my office

Never known love to dig beyond my surface

and

What I know of love has nothing to do with public displays of affection

and what I know of love is that it keeps punching after the bell when I've dropped my shields of protection

What I know of love is only heartbreaks and pain

what I know of love is far too much time spent in vain

I have never known love to visit me or care for me when I'm ill

and I have never known love to embrace me when my heart needs to be healed what do I know of love? absolutely nothing… because, you see

As much as I have given love…it has never been given back to me

but I still dream…

The Hours (Every Time You Go Away)

6pm and...

I cooked your favorite meal
humming the melody of a song you wrote for me
too many years ago
I laugh slightly
remembering a joke you told me
~classic~

Through the kitchen window
sunshine illuminates the dust in your chair
I sit admiring the meticulously set table
suddenly not hungry anymore

The chimes sound the 7 o'clock hour

and I dry my dishpan hands
wander over to the hi-fi and play Donny Hathaway tunes
and if I close my eyes tight enough I could hear your mellow baritone
crooning sweet over the crackling vinyl

For all we know we may never meet again
But before you go make this moment sweet again
We won't say goodnight until the last minute
I'll hold out my hand and my heart will be in it
For all we know this may only be a dream
We come and we go like the ripples of a stream
So love me; love me tonight
Tomorrow was made for some
Tomorrow may never come
For all we know

and I let that familiar warm feeling wash over me
in the darkness
danced longingly with shadows
'til the final glissando faded

...finds me walking from room to room

retracing your footsteps
reliving each memory etched into every space
Can almost hear the laughter
the arguments
the loving
whimsically realizing that walls do talk

I shower around 10

scrubbing roughly
trying to remove your scent from my skin
and I'm still finding your fingerprints splayed boldly
across the expanse of my breast
despite loofah and soap
Tired and raw
I give up

'round midnight

I pull your suit from the closet
-the Armani that fit like an extension of your own skin
carefully matched your tie and shoes
cufflinks, socks, shirt, and watch
All immaculately prepared
Set pristinely upon your pillow
as I snuggle close and fall into restless sleep

There I lay cocooned in stillness
clothed in what used to be
imagining the energy that was
when you still loved me

Love TKO

He saw me from across the street

Walked over as fast as his feet would carry him

I remember dreaming that I would some day marry him

but then…not all dreams come true

but I digress, he asked, "how are you?"

and before I could reply, he let fly his desire to let go of past fires

and let friendship reign and maybe

begin again as confidantes

because he really wants his best friend back.

And for a moment I lost track of time

got lost in the rhythm and rhyme of his request

Who would have guessed I'd ever see him again?

But then, that's how life be

and as a calmness set in, the words came to me.

"I'm better now; better than I was last time we spoke

(slight chuckle). The sound of your voice doesn't cause me to choke up

I've finally erased the last messages you left on my phone

I've stopped shaking uncontrollably when I sit in my home alone.

How am I doing? Well I guess it would suffice to say I'm getting there

I mean

I'm no longer biting my nails or subconsciously pulling out my hair

I am

healing

and no the mention of your name doesn't cause

butterflies to arise in my stomach anymore

and I no longer stare aimlessly at the door

wishing…

hoping…

praying…

pleading with God…

that you would come back to me

Sanity is back within my reach…and

The tremor's almost completely gone from my speech

I no longer break down daily and weep

and I've stopped calling your name and reaching for you in my sleep

I've let go of staying in bed all day long

and screaming in anguish when I hear 'our' song

I'm stronger now than I was back then

I ain't felt this free since I don't know when

but..I can't be your friend

I can't subject myself to talking to you and seeing you like

it's ok

I won't laugh with you and talk with you like I used to

back in the day

It's not that I have hard feelings

I've always wished you the best

I always wanted you to be happy

even when I was going through all that mess

but understand me,

being around you would be like an alcoholic hanging out at a liquor store

or

like a crack-addict spending all his free time with the junkies in the crack house next door

When you left me....

I was broken; completely torn apart

and I thought that death was the only choice I had

to ease the pain in my heart

Hear me clearly

I went through withdrawals when you went away

I damn near lost my mind

couldn't sleep, couldn't eat, couldn't function

I had nightmares of the worst kind

but by the grace of God I made it.

my soul was dying and he saved it.

And I'm not the same woman that you knew

but I still recognize that I can't be around you.

All strong souls have a weakness and mine just happens to be you

so I'm through

pretending that I'm invincible only to get knocked

square on my ass

so while I thank you for your offer of friendship

Please forgive me, but I must pass

Cause not so deeply in my heart,

regardless of what I do

lies a keen awareness that I will never stop loving you

and that's ok...

because my objective was never to throw

all the good memories we have out the door

I just had to learn that no matter how much I love you

I have to love myself even more.

So, it's not personal. I just gotta do what I gotta do

and that means that there is no more room for any kind of 'me and you'

Best of luck. and I truly hope that this life treats you kind

But I have to to say good-bye for good for the sake of my peace of mind.

"I think I better let it go.

looks like another love T.K.O."

Levity

Sometimes this

strong

black

woman

feels more like a

helpless

little

girl

needing just one

strong

black

man

to kiss the hurts away

Gone (No Me 2 Know)

There has never been a time that I did not love you.

Even before I met you, I craved you;

   yearned for you in my soul

Your character etched upon the doorpost of my spirit

Your scent; your touch; your voice all

pre-recorded and stored in the banks of my memory

and the day that I first laid eyes on you...

       I felt a quickening

Though I had never before beheld your face, my soul...

my soul knew who you were; recognized it's mate

Finally a name; a face given to the love that I had waited for

all my life

But you...

       you didn't know me.

I was just a nice girl that you would befriend and like

but you didn't; you couldn't ; you wouldn't

love me.

You taught me how to let go and let you;

schooled me in the finer aspects of pleasure

treasured the way I quickly learned how to please you

how I mastered the ministrations and made you cum..

back for more.

And my soul – seeking recognition and welcome -

sought every imaginable opportunity and avenue to win you

overruled my common sense and

drove me to new depths of desperation

constantly running...

fearing that any base I left uncovered would lead you to seek others

so I emptied out my cup;

poured out every drop of my self-respect, pride, money, shame

gave you everything...

and all I ever wanted in return

was for you to love me back

But you...

you didn't know me.

Drank from my cup until you were full and I was

empty

and then you wandered

listening to the call of other women

who connect to your ego but have no connection

to your soul

and their pomp and circumstance drowns out the

soft sweet melody of my devotion

and I am left standing here

ripped apart; devoid of my sanity

the barest threads of my heart remaining in a

pool of salty tears

trying frantically to piece together the hopes that are now

dashed into a million tiny pieces

my soul…still staring in the distance

calling for you

reaching out for a lifeline to hold on to

but you…

        you didn't know me

And in the silence of my solitude

with my will to live buried beneath my need to not hurt anymore

I give up the ghost.

and now there is no me to know

Spring Cleaning

I found memories of you

wrapped in yellow tissue paper

as delicate as the cashmere and lace

of the indigo sweater I once cherished

and

later an old notebook filled with

he loves me. he loves me not

scribbles

reminded me of the ways

butterflies used to slow drag

to old soul melodies hummed from deep in my belly

long time ago

it was the first time I'd smiled

at a thought of you

since forever

it seems

Time and dust have a way of subtly

letting you know

it wasn't always bad times

love didn't always hurt

and instead of resenting you for the pieces of myself

you took away from me

I learn to appreciate the parts of yourself you left behind

realizing no amount of spring cleaning in the world can erase

the fingerprints you left on my soul

and imagining how those circular ridged smudges

add character to the mosaic of my life

a brushstroke

a solitary blade of grass

perhaps a twinkling silver star

helping to guide me to where I'm supposed to be

so in peace I smooth out yellow tissue paper and

let tattered pages flutter closed

leaving them as a memorial

of what was

and a monument

of what can be

again

Cry

I can hear the faint sound

Of the dam breaking

That sick moan that signals the pressure

Has become too much

The crack and crash of things giving way

And

Falling away

Being swallowed up in gulps

By the waters

That brimmed just shy of spilling over lid

They now seep through pores

And skin and bone

Fill my throat like gall

Choking me 'til I can barely breathe

The struggle is in vain

So I let the walls crumble

And simply break down

And Cry

...The Light (Assignment Piece #1)

Met him 'round the fall of the year

And fell for the ear he gave to my dreams

Seemed he'd travelled lifetimes to be mine

But he didn't

And he wasn't

Doesn't make sense that I didn't see it before

But intuition is often ignored in the light of flattery

Tinged with a smattering of lies

Just game disguised as something genuine

Innuendo woven delicately into a quilt of deceit

Had me completely fooled

Just ...just tools of the trade for his kind

Brotha man trynna find what he wanted

But, haunted by loneliness, he guessed it easier to

lure black butterflies into his net for 'just-in-case' purposes

left me underfed; undornourished

fooling me into thinking I'd flourished under his watchful care

though every time I looked around he wasn't there...

Gave just enough to keep me hopeful of redemption

The way he mentioned blissful visions of forever love

I was simply unaware of the fact that he didn't mean with me

So patiently I waited for the seeds he planted in my ear

To come to fruition

Worked fiendishly; on a mission; to be ready for the harvest

Invested myself in the dream that seemed so close

Yet so far away and that's where it stayed

And it was the days that he made promises to comfort me

That kept me company until

The night came just to prove it all a lie

It's then that those dreams fade and I'm left alone

And lonely

Only to seek company in his empty promises again

And again

And again until the emptiness became too much

And common sense broke loose from the powerful clutch of naiveté

The price I paid was too steep

Cause contrary to popular belief,

Talk..is not cheap.

And I'm filing for emotional bankruptcy

And petitioning to keep my sanity while working

To rebuild my credit…and credibility

And be kept company by my self-respect

Which will never neglect me or leave me lonely

And as I bid ho…farewell

The spell is broken and

And this game of cloak and dagger

Finally comes to an end…thankfully

Because my life depended on it

My love is hinged upon it

And I won't slip up and sleep on it again

This end is my beginning

And losing him was ME winning

A homerun in the final inning

Of the game and like Tina Turner

I walk away with my name

And as long as I've got that

And my dignity, I'll regain my spot on top

And the love in me won't stop just because you didn't appreciate it

It still flows fluidly and is rapidly consumed by a man who it seems

Travelled lifetimes to be mine

And he did

And he is

And he loves to watch his black butterfly stretch her wings and soar

On the winds of his love that he pours abundantly and freely

So I can be strong enough and loved enough and high enough

To lift him up to his rightful place on his throne

God, how I have grown through these seasons

Even through the treason I committed against my heart

Time and time again

But in the end. I rise

So I won't despise the lesson…or the teacher for that matter

I scatter bitterness, like ashes, into the past

And move forward

Right toward

The light.

Never (Assignment Piece # 2)

You never gave me flowers

But gave me countless hours of tears

Which I used to water your path that you might bloom

And

You never kissed me tenderly

Just eagerly groped my body

Squeezing from it a decade of decadent pleasures

Siphoning lust and leaving the meaty substance of me

As refuse to be discarded

And

You never said I love you

Though you cleverly skirted the issue with the misuse of

"love is an action…not a word" which is absurd because it's both

And you didn't espouse either

But that's neither here nor there

'cause I was always aware of the truth

Even when I pretended not to be

And

You never imagined me leaving

But I'm gone

And your song is a melody long since forgotten

You just lost one

And you ask 'how come'

And I say

You never gave me flowers

You never kissed me tenderly

You never said I love you...

But he did

Make You Free...

The truth has a way of

Seeping through the cracks

And finding the light

Despite our futile efforts to

Hide it

Suppress it

See it's a living thing

Breathing and moving

And it fights for dear life

When you try as you might to bury it

Digs its way out for all to see

While you stand idly by

And watch your house of lies

Crumble beneath its weight

It's no way to live

No way to flourish

You cannot grow in the shadows of doubt

You cannot spread your wings and fly in the clutches of a lie

Why not just live in the light?

In the bright sunshiny beams of the truth

What have you got to lose but your soul

Be bold with yours

If you want to go, say so!

It's sad though, that you have no reason to lie to me

Yet you do

Which leads me to believe I have no clue of who, or what, you are anymore

But I implore you to bask in the warmth of day

Because betrayal of your conscience is too big a price to pay

For secrets that have no consequence

But lies that do

And ye shall know the truth, and the truth shall make you free – John 8:32

Love

Self

No More Tears

I've resolved it in my heart that I will shed

No more tears for the men who took up too many of my years

We hold this truth to be self-evident that

I will not cry or lament a relationship that was never meant

Any man who breaks my heart is not worthy of being a part

Of my life

I am wife material and no serial manipulator can make the mess I've been through

Greater than my destiny

There is a husband for me even if it's only the Almighty

I no longer cast my pearls before swine

Or pine away aimlessly for men who shamelessly use me

Or choose to be with another

The brother just did me a favor and saved me the labor

Of swimming in the shark infested waters of his heart

Where I would be torn apart at the seams

and the one I deemed the man of my dreams would only

cause nightmares

I declare war on my insecurities and I am finally free to just be

RareEpiphany

Natural hair

Dark skin

Wide azz and all

I will no longer fall prey to your fantasies

For my reality is far greater

Stare boldly in the mirror and scream "Take Her!..."

Or leave her for that matter 'cause it really don't matter

Your absence or presence won't shape or shatter the woman that I am

'cause I'll be damned to an eternal hell before I sell my soul

Or be controlled by another man again

And that's not the end of love

No, no

Love can now begin

IN me

With me

Through me

With clarity

I now see the fallacies

That clouded my thinking

And drinking at this well-spring of understanding

Has me singing redemption songs that had long since been

Hushed by the gag of emotional slavery that was yoked upon me

Not long after infancy when my innocence was stolen and

a seed of self-hatred sown in me

And a tree of regrets took root, grew, and bore fruit

That lacked the sweetness of self-esteem and the firmness of resolve

And all those leaves of discontent blocked my view of the horizon

And if I'd only seen the sun….or felt the Son this metamorphosis would have begun

Long ago

But I know that greatness is born of struggle

And sometimes it takes juggling too many things

And dropping things to know that broken things don't mean

The breaking of me.

I'm made of tougher stuff

And there ain't enough hurt on this earth to bring me down

So haters just have to drown in my spit

Cause I've resolved it and made it crystal clear

Right now and right here that I will shed

No

More

Tears

Independence Day
(Woman In The Mirror)

I used to hate her...me

the woman in the mirror

I hated her so deeply that once (or twice)

I tried to kill her.

I hated her laughter

(it was fake 'cause she was never really happy)

I despised her dreams

(because I knew that she had never been nor would ever be "somebody")

How dare she fool herself?

There are no dreams for poor black fat girls

there is no fame or love...

They celebrate what she does

but scoff at who she is

So she does more and more and more

'cause when the curtain goes down

there is no one

the applause goes silent

and she sits alone in utter darkness

'til the next show...

Somewhere in her celebrity she had lost her humanity

and I hated her for it.

She wasn't a woman. She was a puppet.

And the rejection of male-kind

and the casual conceit of female-kind

reminded her every day that

she was no prize to any man

nor threat to any woman

        just a song and dance in the nighttime

She allowed herself to be used and discarded like...

like...tissue...like gum

chewed until they lost the taste for her...me

The woman in the mirror.

And I wished I never met her at all, at all.

'Til one morning, I looked up into her sad eyes

and wept for her

pitied her

let myself feel compassion for her

screamed in rage and heartbreak for her

brushed away her tears for her

I healed for her

And before I could stop myself

I found myself falling in love with her...me

The woman in the mirror

For the first time, I saw something beautiful

beyond the hurt.

I saw HER

and I fell so in love…

And I celebrate that day.

My Independence Day

The day I accepted dark chocolate skin

and nappy black hair

The day I gained an appreciation for full lips

broad nose and muddy brown eyes

It was the day I became whole

I had to see the good in me

embrace the bad in me

and ratify the originality of

this temple; this soul

I saw wide hips and I loved them

'cause brothas stare when I walk away

I winked at thick thighs

whose smooth sumptuous texture cushion my love's journey

to the pleasures of my paradise

I blew kisses at full breasts

that will one day feed life to the fruit of my womb

and lust the man of my dreams

And I touched…caressed my soft middle where memories of

grandma's biscuits, daddies bbq , mama's candied yams, and still-born dreams

echo through my being

"I love you." I whispered to her…me

The woman in the mirror;

to my heart;

to my soul;

"I love you…I love all of you"

Me

The woman in the mirror

Somewhere

There's a song in me

Somewhere

I can't find it right now

The melody is lost in the loudness of my every day

But I know it's there

Waiting

Playing softly in the chaotic cacophony

Beneath my cries for help

and my grocery lists

behind my 9 to 5 or 6 or 10

underneath potty training frustration

and toys and tantrums and laundry

There is a song in me

Somewhere

It just got lost in the shuffle and now lay

Buried in the rubble of my existence

But soon

I will find it

I will shed the tears and hush the worries

I will resign myself to the fact that the ends will never meet

And that there is no 'right time'

Only 'right now'

And I will sit down and calm down

And dig down into the very depths and unearth

My music

'cause there is a song in me

Somewhere

Just waiting

To be sung

Love Rains / Reigns

Love Rains…

Like tears from heaven

And the mellifluous flow of

Music from Donny Hathaway's mouth

Crackling sweet on vinyl

~Timbre smooth like

Honeysuckle breezes after

Love-rains…

Drips warm from brown eyes

Trickles cool down soft cheeks

To heal

To assuage the pain of sutured hearts

A balm for spirit-wounds

Love Reigns

Rightly

With reborn conviction

A phoenix from the darkness

Bending rainbows across fresh azure skylines

As a sign to the universe that the curse

Is broken

And

Love Reigns Here

Evermore

Now Found (The Woman I Could Be)

He said he wanted to talk so, without a second thought

I gave him my number

had no reason for trepidation

After all

This was just about friendly conversation

So

Robed in confidence, I spoke freely

But it wasn't confidence in me, but my truths that

Blew like breeze through fiber optic lines

See, my mind was the draw

And if that's all he saw, then it was enough

Such things as love were not meant for me

So I was confident, you see

In the fact that this playful back and forth

Banter was a decanter for nothing more than conversation

No strings

No hopes

No wishful thinking

Just deciphering the inking of words on the prison of my insecurity

Masked brilliantly as a castle of dreams

This seemed almost text book in its inception

With the exception of his smile

I could feel it over the phone

Over the keystrokes

Over the miles

Between us

But I just dismissed it as a gem in the crown of his mystique

And continued to keep things light

With the heavy things of life nestled within our poetry

Speaking deeply and philosophically about

Realms beyond this marble of clay

Flung into space we called home

Roamed the recesses of each others minds

Didn't know that I'd find what I wasn't looking for

Love

And I tried to close the door but still it seeped

Through the cracks, filled every empty space with its sweetness

'til it surrounded me and confounded my every preconceived idea

Here I was laying poems at his feet when what he wanted was for me

To lay my heart in his hands

And though I ran, he'd sought me

Came after me and caught me

Pulled me from my chrysalis

And lay me bare

And none the wiser was I 'til

he made me see the future in the reflecting pools of his eyes

I peered deeply and suddenly I fell in love

With me

I saw what he sees each time he looks at me

Beneath hair and skin and blood and bone

Marrow deep; the heart of me

Couldn't believe I'd missed her

All this time

And that very moment I vowed to cherish her

And never forsake her

Care for her and never take her for granted

Candid glances revealed imperfections

But to me, she was a brilliantly vivid confection of triviality and gravity

And the tapestry of her life hung boldly across the sky

Wild and beautiful and free

And I fell in love with the woman that I am

On the day he introduced me to the woman I could be

The Blessing of Writer's Block..

Looking out of my window

Indigo sky waxes fluid like midnight seas

And somewhere in the moon's pale glow

Is a poem

Murky, but there nonetheless

Speaking, but in whispers I can only hear in my dreams

…Blank pages in my lap

..Pen stilled and dry

I smile and watch

Content to read what God has written upon the sky

Inside Out

It's gray outside

But the light in my soul outshines any rays the sun could hope to extend to earth

My smile; an inverted rainbow stretching across my face and down into the heart of me

Where lies a treasure far weightier than gold

And somewhere inside, thoughts run free

Taking advantage of the recesses of my mind

Swinging into blue oasis and

Sifting through the sands of time

With happy tears

Mingling the two and creating castled monuments of this 'right now'

And yes, history has proven that there's an ocean out there

Filled with predators seeking to destroy

And waves of adversity have been known to crash upon the shores

Beating down dreams created on days like this

But that is neither here nor there

For we are Here and NOW

So until….

Until….

I will let my thoughts run wild and free

I will let myself envision me and you and us

Living this moment for eternity

Second by second

Hour by hour

Day by day

And come what may

We always have 'right now'

What we have to do

Is remember it

When 'then' comes

Hairy Cane

He asked me what I was going through

See he couldn't understand the new 'me'

I guess I shouldn't be surprised

'cause as of late all eyes had been on me

I had changed.

Once quiet breeze now Hairycane..

I refrained from chemically altering my hair

How dare I be free?

"your hair used to be so pretty"

Was all they could say the day I walked in

Rockin' two strand twists

Twisted their minds one mo' time

With silk locs but no I wouldn't stop there

Scared them straight when corn rows draped my shoulders

Made bolder by the black wooden beads engraved with free...'huru' in Swahili

They can't see the beauty in that

Not the flyness of my headwraps or the

Love I see in my naps

Kinked up and fro'd out

I'm much more concerned about the content of my character

Rather than the straightness of my mane

Had to retrain my own thinking as to what this queen's crown should look like

And despite the pressure from company execs.

They truly expected a tete-et-tete to intimidate me into who I used to be

I just smiled

Raised my arched brow

Leaned in uncomfortably close

And said hell no

My 'fro has nothing to do with my work

But everything to do with who I am

And I gives a dayum about your promotions

Or your Eurocentric notions about what success looks like

Are my figures right?

Do my calculations sync?

They do? Then worry less about my naps and kinks

And more about the caliber of my labor

Do me a favor and weigh my conscious cloud against the way I've allowed

The demands of my vocation to take over my vacations and the countless hours

From home that I've droned away at my tasks and not even asked you for the overtime that is

Rightfully mine.

So I decline your offers of assimilation and remain in the station

You've relegated for me as "not a team player" while you give your

"There is no "I" in team" spiel

But let's keep it real, there's no "u" in team either. You fail to see the true meaning

Of the word.

It's 4 different letters coming together for one purpose; to create something that cannot be created

by each letter alone…but please hone in on the catcher

no 2 letters are the same

Rather, they are all unique and don't change themselves to complete the task of building a word

So it's absurd to think that in order to be team we have to all be the same

Or look the same

Or think the same

you need my hairycane to shake this thang' up!

I've given up way too much of myself already

So what you see right now

Is what you get and if that doesn't work, then go find your Stedfort

Employee and let me go.

Cause I know who I am

and that's not going to change

not your quiet breeze

you'll see me coming

Hairycane

In the 'doing' (dancing at night)

I dance in the nighttime

where no eyes, but God's bare witness

And the miracle that transpires in my heart

Is my and my savior's business

It is of no consequence to me

whether you see

the beauty of my dance

because I've learned that the peace is in the `doing'

I don't need an audience

and when I dance...I belt out my spirit song...I pour out my everything

and just because you don't hear my music

doesn't mean that I don't sing.

I cry in the dark.

where razor sharp memories

pierce the murky depths of my soul

though my smile belies my struggle

and I seem to have it all in control

it gets hard sometimes but I chose to only tell

the One on whom I can depend

and nobody sees my tears

but me.

But that doesn't mean they don't cleanse

My heart aches with the pain of loss

and it's been tossed around a time or two

it's been bruised...and it's been shattered

into thousands of fragmented and tattered pieces

and peace is constantly evading its grasp

and smiling through the rain has become a task that...

ain't easy

please see that though you cannot picture my pain and stress

It doesn't mean it hurts any less

and I've been blessed to see sunshine on the darkest of days

and I've been highly favored in a multiplicity of ways

and though you may not see my wonder when I watch the sun's rays

it doesn't at all mean that I'm not utterly amazed

Understand, though I don't yet perform before millions of fans

it doesn't mean I'm not blessed with talent

For the skills and gifts God has given me run the creative gamut

But they were never endowed to win me the praises of men

but in the event that it happens....well then.. that's icing on the cake

My take on the situation is that He gave that I might be fulfilled

that through the light He's given me, my weary soul might be healed

I am what He made me

I reflect what He imparts

and if nobody ever sees me

it doesn't change the display of my art

See, the sun shines because that's what it was made to do

It rises and sets everyday regardless of me or you

Its course is set by the Master of the sky

And it does not question. It does not ask why

whether any one acknowledges its warmth or its beauty

is of no relevance...it lives to fulfill its duty

to shine...even when hidden by clouds

to radiate...even when there're storms for miles

And like the sun...I keep on shining

Keep on laughing

Keep on crying

keep on singing

keep on writing

keep on reaching

keep on trying

It is of no consequence to me

whether you see

the beauty of my dance

because I've learned that the peace is in the `doing'

and I don't need an audience

10 Minutes (Dam Won't Break)

It's 10 minutes 'til midnight

and this dam won't break

winds of strife blow through my mind

scattering thoughts prismatic

'til the brilliance blinds me

and all I see are rainbows

bending over the aftermath

flood waters lurch and build

but still

it's 10 minutes 'til midnight

and this dam won't break

Didn't think I could withstand the pressure

of these swolling tides that got my eyes

bleeding and weakened

but pride refuses to be pushed aside

spite stands strong against the surge

cracks sutured with blood and sweat

but no tears

there are none here

Regrets march 'round my Jericho wall

& amidst all the sound and fury I think

Surely it will crumble….surely it will break

Cause I can't take another 7 days in this maze

Where is Grace when I am in need

Somebody please intercede for me

'cause you see it's 10 minutes 'til midnight

And this dam won't break

And though I'm scared, I wish it would just break through

I feel so unprepared but I want it to just break through

Don't even think I can survive but please just let it break through

I'm so desperately in need of a breakthrough

but I stand alone

stronger than I ever wanted to be

waiting for this flood to overtake me

mercifully

and though it's 10 minutes 'til midnight

and this dam won't break

I pray that

soon it will

They Thought They Knew Me (Ego Trippin' part 2)

…They thought they knew me

blew me off as just another poet

whose spirit is gentle and kind

behind this screen I seemed like a

queen/mother/sister girl type

that carried around the hype of

'peace and blessings' and head-dressing

smokin' cess and that type of mess

but I guess I should have told them

that this gem ain't cut like the rest

so just in case there's been some confusion

the conclusion to the matter is this:

I am Mrs. and Miss

been known to use my fists

and it's not a boast

but moot know not to mess with me

I'm silly and serious

hypocrites make me furious

I'm a lover and fighter

a reader and a writer

some think my flow is tighter than the average scribe

while others decide they're just not feeling my vibe

and that …well that simply don't bother me

cause at the end of the day, it's all subjective

My perspective is just to do what I do

I am defined by the Creator and aim to please Him not the many or the few

See I am more than human

I'm uniquely divine

Just like everyone else – I am one of a kind

I am more than passion

more than poetry and prose

more than the degrees I hold

more than friend or foe

 you can't box me up or label me

I exude the very essence of individuality

both bitch and saint

bright but faint

both virgin and whore

for the core of sexuality is more than the physical

it's spiritual

and the biblical term for intimacy is to 'know'

and no man has known me yet so behold

a miracle of lyrical dissension

For I am a contradiction in perfect agreement with myself

I cannot be silenced or put on the shelf

I am a multi-dimensional prismatic allegory

and if you read everything by or about me you still wouldn't know my story

I'm deeper than the written word

more expansive than any language

I far surpass the things you've heard

Defy the intellect of the minds at Cambridge

Make no mistake, I am cerebral and emotional

The sum of my parts can't even touch my total

I am infinity wrapped up in infinity

with an affinity for all that Divinity has to offer me

I am a mystery

of epic proportions

enlightening minds sick with distortions of the truth

I am living proof of 'what don't kill you can only make you stronger'

I am the secret addiction that men can no longer hide

The pride of the ages and shame of the nation

Administer of healing and in-need-of-healing patient

I'm the tale that will go down in history

No matter my good my name lives in infamy

made wonderfully and fearfully

A beautifully unperformed symphony

I am

simply

and gently

without apology

RareEpiphany

Love

Making

Home ~ The Deep Down of Me

It started in the

Deep down of me

The deep warm brown of me

Where none but love and your lust can touch.

To whom much is given

Much is required

And I aspire to open myself

Ocean wide

Then you can slide into

The deep down of me

The deep warm brown of me

And get off on the sound of me

Ushering you inside of me with praises

While my face is the picture of passion

And my hips skillfully fashioned to take it

How you give it

~Deep~

Down

Past the

Brown of me

In the very black of me

Damn near middle passage savagery

or could it be

~plantation relations~

when you loved like it was the last time

cause it could very well be the last time.

My fingers clutch your spine and

I breathe in sync with yo grind

And the only thing on my mind

Is 'please daddy take yo time'

And find the

Deep

So deep

Down brown of me

So I can cry yo name

When you're deep inside of me

And you'll know without doubt that you have found in me

A place called home

Lick

~ *(HANDle)* ~

You watch me;

read the story unfolding behind my eyes;

take note of every twitch of my jaw

…quiver of my lips;

Studying, diligently, every subtle nuance of

My flesh…

      My breathing…

           My voice

Your touch

Responds to my call

Slowly…gently playing me

Like a maestro on piano

You quicken…when my body beckons

Then, mastering me, you

Take control of my rhythm

Directing…

      Guiding…

           Soliciting…

The look…sound…movement you want

Coaxing me to the brink

Teetering on the edge 'til I beg

But you don't let me fall…yet

You watch me;

the masterpiece before you

a living breathing portrait of passion

then you...

push me over into ecstasy

spread my thighs

...sigh

And then

~Lick~

Can't Hide Love

You're not fooled by the calmness of my exterior

Though my gaze holds yours steadily

And the rise and fall of my chest is smooth…almost calculated

You see it….

The heat and desire pooling just beneath the surface of my cocoa skin

The faint traces of sweat forming subtly along my brow

You smile slyly at the quivering pulse point on my neck

And slowly lick your lips

The hitch in my breathing doesn't go unnoticed.

You speak…about everything and nothing

But I don't hear a single word you say

I just follow the hypnotic movement of your lips

Fighting the urge to touch them with butterfly fingers

Lick them with lithe tongue and then suck their honey brown fullness

Until you moan my name

I exhale

Only then realizing that I'd been holding my breath at the thoughts that weighed

So heavily on my mind that they left imprints that are taking much too long to fade

I want you

~And you know it~

In the best and the nastiest of ways

In the deep down low and ride you slow kinda ways

The back seat of a caddy "just f*ck me daddy!" kinda ways

In the up against the wall until the pictures all fall kinda ways

I want you

And from the look in your eyes

I can tell you

Want me

Too

Just Breathe

I can't breathe

when you look at me that way

You don't have to say a word

and still my body heard the whisper in your eyes

and a quiver slithers up my thighs

and I lose my breath at the depth

of desire thick in your gaze

amazed at how you make me want to dance naked to the bolero

rhythm you cause my heart to beat

and heat seeps through my veins; melting candy that rains

in thick creamy drops from my honey pot that you keep

boiling over and then your eyes slip lower

over my full brown breasts

and satisfaction at how the nipples strain towards you

causes the evidence of your arousal to press hard against your zipper

I grip your hands and slide them over my belly

you tell me to keep moving

while your fingers are slow grooving over my hips

and then slip into my slick abyss and pull jazz riffs from my throat

and I float on Congo drums ignited by the

slow hum you churn in my core

and I beg for more when you kneel on the floor

and orally explore my middle passage

and savage instincts to scream against an azure sky

and ride your tongue 'til I cum jordan rivers

that baptized you into new life rise to new heights within me

and I can't breathe

when you look at me that way

my release on your face

eyes dark and glazed

arms raised beckoning me

to your embrace

and I meet you

in that place between time and eternity

and then you breathe for me

through me

inside me

freeing me to breathe for myself

so when you're left breathless, I press my lips to yours

exhale and then grip my nails in your back

and wrap my legs tightly around your waist and with haste

rotate my hips 'til your control slips

and you drip living waters into my soul

then you slowww...ly

with me

in sweet peace

just

breathe

Memory Lane

I'm travelling back

down

memory lane

to a night in February…68 degrees with light drizzling rain

but inside….it was 100 plus

cause when I'm alone with you

heat and humidity is a must

you just….do that to me

and that night I couldn't have adequately anticipated

the way our feelings would be communicated

it was surreal

the look in your eyes spoke volumes incessantly

the way you touched me whispered you wanted me

as we spoke in tongues with our tongues

entangled

and we dangled dangerously on the edge

of animal behavior

I still taste the salty-sweet flavor

of the nape of your neck

and

still feel the cool trickle of

glistening beads of sweat

I shiver as I recall the soft warmth of your breath snaking down my spine causing all of my protests to spill off my tongue as whimpers and whines

for…

"…oooh sì…più.. il mio amore"

and I tried so hard to control the trembling that began

in my legs

and I couldn't stop the screams of ecstasy

no matter how fiercely I gripped the bed

Could barely make out your voice in my ear or your

soft, yet demanding invitation to…cum

had no control over the tears that fell as you made

my body hummmm

And when I opened myself wider to receive you deeper

and moaned your name repeatedly in your ear

the low guttural growl that escaped from betwixt your clenched teeth

caused all sanity to disappear

I lost my mind in the grind of your fine as wine hips

I lost my resistance in the insistence and urgency of your lips

I lost my fear and doubt with each in and out on the floor and couch and bed

I lost my association with articulation for there was no translation for what I said

…we were Kinetic – energy in motion

so thoroughly charged that we set off millions of explosions

and I live to tell the story

of love making so intense

that it took me 9 months, 1 week, 3 days and 8 hours

to write anything about it that made any sense.

Body Music

Last night we made body music

limbs entangled

dancing to the steady

suck/slide rhythm

of hips in overdrive

accented by the percussive scratching of sheets

springs singing staccato to the

headboard's driving kick

made perfect by the syncopated knocks of

neighbors on walls

begging for decrescendo

but artisans that we are,

we...

Da Capo

From the beginning again

this time legato

tonguing each note expertly

bringing in congo lines

charmed hips subtly

undulate

churning; churning

it's butter baby

hands sliding along ribcage

fingers caressing each bone like

harp strings

or more like

keys on a baby grand

and baby damn how you

play so smooth and slow

the barely audible grip of fingers on moist skin

fades into the whisper soft backdrop

of sighs and moans

then warm licked lips

slip low and play my flute

rubato

driving hard to crescendo

tongue conducts slow arching of back

salsa y meringue

throaty alto once dolce

now rings Sforzando

this is body music

and tears flow and

alto modulates to sharp soprano

then

~consonance~

found in the ragged breaths of 2 musicians

finally completing

lovers' brown-skinned symphony

Nights Like This

On nights like this

I dream of

skinny dipping in the amber pools of your eyes

bathing in your gaze and watching son's set on your horizon

I run along your brown sand beaches

enjoying the feel of dampness that comes after

the tearful rains

and on nights like this

I dream of the scent of your warm moist skin

inhale again and again the masculine zen cupped in your collarbone

take slow sips of sweet chocolate

languishing lavish licks on the back of your neck

try hard to keep in check the slow simmer consuming me

and you make it hard, you see, cause you moan my name so

deliciously that I subsequently almost forget to be good

I exhale slowly

as I try to get steady

on my feet

but you greet my retreat with advances

and sensual glances over your shoulder

coupled with hands that grow bolder by the minute

make eminent my demise

what I see in your eyes makes me tremble

and it nimbly removes my inhibitions

as you switch positions to face me

and I see the breadth and depth of your hunger for me

my eyes plead for mercy

but you show none

and I'm undone as I slowly run my hands over your chest

let them rest on your ribcage as I engage

in slow, sensual, French kisses

on your nipples

desire ripples through your body

pinning me between a rock and a

very hard place

brace for the tidal waves about to hit my shore

as bodies hit floor

scream for more

while on all fours

shaken to my core

and honey love pours

all over us

just melting into molten pools of pleasure…and

On nights like this

I dream that your kiss

fixes all of my broken places

fills all of my empty spaces

and erases all those bad memories etched on the walls of my soul

It's nights like this

when halves are made whole

It's nights like this when dreams come true

and on nights like this

I dream

about you

He's Cumming For Me

Right now...it doesn't matter If the sky shatters

or stars scatter like confetti to the ground

I've found peace in the space between

his moans and the earth-tones of our damp skin

something akin to tribal dances advance from our hips

and we take slow sips of lust

and if right now I be thrust into an ever after missing the chapters

to a happy ending

I'll still be sending candy kisses to the sun

because the one thing that does matter

is that he's cumming for me

and I can see the eminent arrival in his eyes

and the way he grips my thighs tells me he's close

and the most beautiful sound escapes his throat

and I feel the remote trembling that emanates from a place

so primitive and deep that it reaches peaks at rock bottoms

Autumn's turned to spring and everything cold is now hot

and I forgot the meaning of the universe when he softly

cursed the wave about to overtake him and me

and history is repeating itself and self control is beating itself

and I don't give a damn cause I am weathering the storm

in the safety of his arms and

he's cumming for me

white waters run rapidly

tempos increase and I succumb to the slow heat

of his piston-like motions

drowning his steel adrenaline in my sticky wet ocean

he takes me fast and hard

threatening to rip me apart but my heart won't let me stop

reaching desperately for that mountain top

and it doesn't matter that my mind's locked in a pleasure-pain trap

and it doesn't matter that my body lies at the brink of collapse

or that in the distance my fragile soul hears strains of taps

What does matter is the faint quiver of his lips

and the way he pants in steady succinct sips

and I squeeze my thighs tightly around his hips

and rock my backside in the jagged rhythm of his grip

He is cumming for me and that reality

rivals my every fantasy and I am happy to be there

when he arrives

Mind Grindin'

You seem like the kind of man

that can treat a woman like a lady

but maybe tonight

I want to be treated like your girl

…there's a world of difference

and while I freely admit

that I wish to lick tears from your eyes

as I ride you

slow-ly

and drape me lavishly across your body

Please believe that it's your mind-flow

that got my nose open

and I'm hoping that you'll open my soul wide

and slide your thoughts inside

pushing deep into my mind

with a prolific poetic slow grind

and find my spot

that dot of space that you can hit

and erase all my past lives

all those past lies

all those past ties

to untruths I courted in my youth

Mind-f*ck me 'til I buck free

of the shackles that bind me

'til I beg for mercy cause your verbs are killing me

with their steady in and out

'til I shout multi-syllabic adjectives like they were expletives

and scream superlatives never-minding my fricatives

or plosives

exposed is my very core

when I plead for more and you explore my intellect

with your silver tongue

plunge into me lyrically like a delicacy

Rewriting me with long deliberate strokes

and I spoke you in metaphors

repeat you like the "nevermore"

from Poe's raven

Brazenly cravin' your di-dac-dic....

flow

It grows more rigid the more you give it to me

I see moonflowers as I devour every utterance of your mouth

your down-south skillz got me head over heals

stanzas building to crescendo verses laced with innuendo

you throw your back into it as you spew fluid word-music

and I lose it and scream...I lose it and cream ink all over my sheets

of loose-leaf

you released soliloquies that dripped from me like honey

You've done me and I am complete

and my heart beats a melody for you

my mouth pants a rhythmic groove

and my shaking fingers grasp your bic

my tongue flicks the tip …I tighten my grip

dip my hips and with a

slip of my wrist

I twist limericks

between lip-licks

pulling hat tricks with quick-witted precision

like a piston until you blast ink in a passionate blink of my 3rd eye

and I try not to spill a drop but it drips

from my lips in the sweetest haiku's

and doiditsu's spew forth like summer rain

can't contain those triolets

that got me wet and kyrielles keep me in a

purple haze

we make it do what it do

and I got the sweetest love jones for making poetry

With you

The Kiss

He looked through my too brown eyes

and not-so-perfect skin

directly into my soul

stepped closer into my

comfort zone 'til my world was thrown off kilter

He filtered out my excuses and explanations

and with a surgeons precision patience

He found me

Carved through this caricature to find my character

and then after a long moment I averted my eyes

'cause he'd seen through my disguise

and I was naked

My sacred spaces were hidden no more

and my imperfections lay scattered on the floor

of my cutting room

Doomed to be known in their entirety

and then silently he

lifted my chin

looked into those too brown eyes again

butterflies in my stomach dance and spin

heartbeats flutter and pound within

As he gently pulled me by my too thick waist

and placed his lips on mine

took his time inhaling my exhales

my thoughts failed as he

drank me in sips

slowly tasted my lips

savored their too full decadence

and I lost sense of time

as he reminded me that I was woman

and from inside I heard music

as he licked the lining of my mouth

I moan deliciously "uhmm" when he

suckles my bottom lip just before he dips

inside and my tongue guides him into the safety of my palate

And I caress him there as he strokes my hair

and I know beyond doubt

that I am loved.

Again…

I want you

I want you deep

I want you deep inside

I want you deep inside of me

…My hands

…My mouth

…My walls

…My mind

…My heart

…My spirit

Strong and free and deep

Fulfilling me while you are feeling me

Completely

We are sensually linked

And no pen in the world can ink the depth of what happens

To my body when you speak breathlessly in my ear

And my fear is that this dam will overflow the very moment

You touch me

Like something tantric

And I will franticly grasp for an anchor

To keep me steady

My orgasm stands ready at the threshold

To unfold and boldly slither up my spine

And find my voice

Shaking loose choice words of intense passion

Something dirty in the fashion of porn stars

Or sailors in seedy bars

Or maybe just a low lingering moan

 To signal that your touch has found a home

On my skin

And I might spin again and again into

Multiple rhythmic reactions

By no other actions than your breath on my neck

Cause I can't keep in check the energy you release in me

When you simply speak my name

Can't tame the vixen you awaken in I

No matter how hard I try

So I surrender to the bend of your back

And the oral attack of your spoken word

And utter verbs reserved for private places

As your poetic penchant erases the line between

Fantasy and reality

Cause really….

The physicality of what you do to me

Is easily surpassed by the

Amazingly simple things you say to me

And I willingly give you all of me

And that's a scary thing

So touch me gently

And ignite my soul

And I promise to surrender control

And touch you back

So when you lose track of time and find yourself

Behind schedule

And all of your professional friends ask where you've been

Tell them you were lost deep inside an Epiphany

Drowning in a Rarity so deliciously

Pressed tightly between peaks of divine revelation

Practicing the fine art of mental penetration

Then close your eyes and smile wickedly

Breathe to relieve passion's urgency

Then go about your day knowing the night will soon begin

And you can return to my embrace where I can touch you

Again

Coda

www.ingramcontent.com/pod-product-compliance
Lightning Source LLC
Chambersburg PA
CBHW020913090426
42736CB00008B/609